Paper Planes

...to make and fly

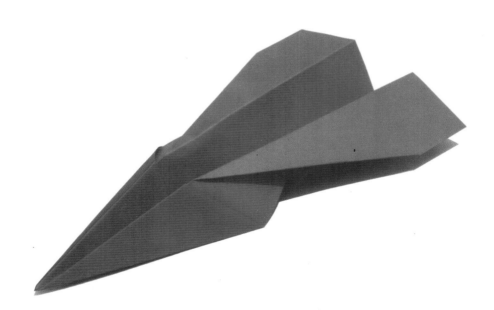

Paper Planes

...to make and fly

Nick Robinson

D&S
BOOKS

© 2007 D&S Books Ltd

D&S Books Ltd
Kerswell,
Parkham Ash, Bideford
Devon, England
EX39 5PR

e-mail us at:-
enquiries@dsbooks.fsnet.co.uk

This edition printed 2007

ISBN 13 – 978-1-903327-49-4

Book Code: DS0159. Paper Planes

Material from this book previously appeared in Paper Planes.

Creative Director: Sarah King
Photographer: Colin Bowling
Designer: Dynamo Limited, Exeter

Printed in Thailand

1 3 5 7 9 10 8 6 4 2

Contents

Introduction

The sight of an airplane passing overhead is commonplace these days, yet people still look upwards and watch with fascination as these gleaming machines speed towards their destination. Where does it come from? Where is it going? Who is on board? We know none of these things, yet the simple fact that they are in the air seems to make their trip mysterious and exotic.

For most people, airplanes are a fact of life and have always been there, yet the first flight was just 100 years ago. Despite our best efforts, man cannot fly without a machine to help him. However, we can still make other things fly; balloons, gliders, parachutes, and best of all, paper planes

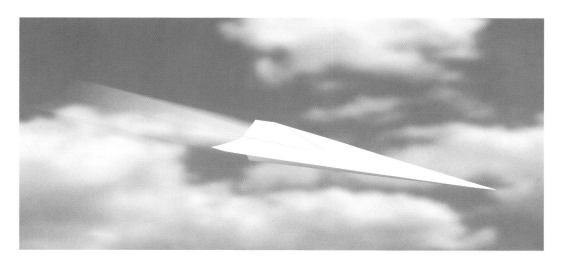

Introduction

We don't know when the first paper plane was invented, but the classic 'dart' seems to be over 100 years old. It may have predated the first real plane! As with most paper folding (often known as 'origami'), the economy of means is a major attraction. You only need paper and your hands and within 30 seconds or so, you can create something that can take to the skies. Since they have no engine, paper planes can glide at best. This means they won't stay in the air for long. The current world record for time in the air is less than 30 seconds. One of the designs in this book may well beat that record if you are prepared to practise and experiment!

This book aims to take the design of paper planes a small step forward. New techniques for 'locking' the sides of the plane together are used and you are recommended to experiment and extend these ideas. One truth about paper-folding is that just when you think all of the good ideas and designs have already been discovered, somebody finds a new one and you think, 'I wish I'd thought of that!' New ideas are waiting in the paper to be discovered with no more than basic folding skills, some imagination and a bit of dedication.

How to create an 'A' proportion rectangle

Many of the planes in this book are best made from A4 sized paper. This is easily made from either a square or any other rectangle, as shown below.

'A' proportion from a rectangle

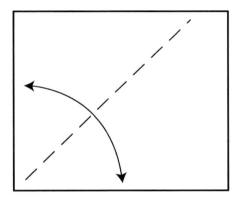

1 Fold one side to an adjacent side, crease and unfold

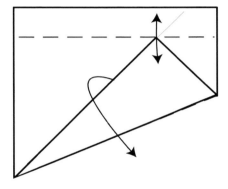

3 Fold the top edge over, making a crease that touches the corner-crease and unfold

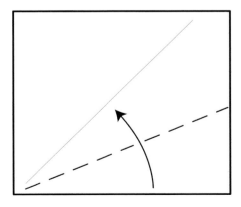

2 Fold the lower edge to the crease

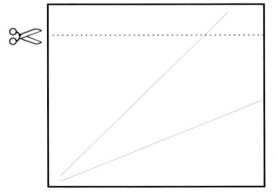

4 Cut along the crease

Introduction

'A' proportion from a square

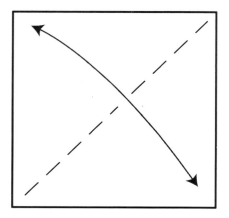

Fold one side to an adjacent side, crease and unfold

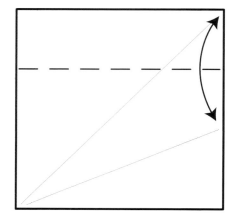

Fold the top edge over to meet the end of the crease made in the last step- crease and unfold

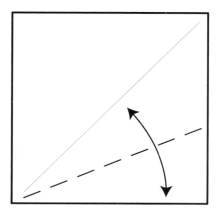

Fold the lower edge to the crease

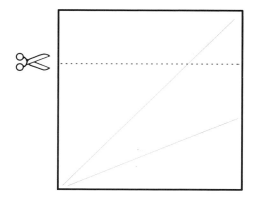

Cut along the crease

Paper planes are usually very lightweight and so are easily affected by wind. The only sensible answer to this problem is to fly your planes indoors and keep all windows and doors shut. Good locations include gymnasiums, halls, large garages, and so on. An ideal location has no wind or draughts, a length of 300 feet and a height of 100 feet. The only place you can find this is in sports arenas or aircraft hangars, which can prove expensive to hire, but it is worth it. You can then break some world records!

Paper has a tendency to absorb moisture from the air. This means your plane's wings will start to sag after a while. There is no cure for this (other than a warm, dry room) so you should be prepared to 'retire' your plane after a fairly limited lifespan. You should then fold another! The frustrating part is that no matter how carefully you fold two apparently identical planes, one may be a great flier, the other hopeless. This is part of the fun, since if it were easy to predict flight characteristics, the whole process would become mechanical. The reality of the situation is that a raw beginner can strike lucky and get very impressive results.

Introduction

Optional Extras

Many paper plane enthusiasts are quite strict when making paper planes; they will only use folding techniques to achieve their results. Others will use sticky tape, weights, cuts, extra pieces, anything it takes to help the plane fly. The rules for the paper plane world record (both for distance and for time in the air), allow you to use small pieces of tape to keep the wings together.

A few years ago, following a suggestion from the British Origami Society, a new category was added, which insists on the use of pure origami techniques with no cuts or use of tape. This has encouraged many paper-folders to have a go at designing paper planes: some of the exciting designs are featured within this book. Many children like to tear small flaps in the wings to make it look better and possibly improve the flight. The use of flaps can certainly allow you to make fine adjustments to the 'trim' of the plane, but you may feel that it is less satisfactory than 'pure' folding.

Everyone has his or her own standards and you should do whatever makes you happy! It is also true that adding some weight to the front end of a plane (in the form of a paper clip) will often make it fly better, but you may think that is a bit of a cheat.

Tips for folding from this book

1   Make sure your hands are clean before folding!

2   Fold on a flat surface, such as a table.

3   Don't rush the model - fold slowly, carefully and neatly.

4   If you don't quite understand the photos, read the words as well.

5   Make each plane three times - the last should fly much more effectively than the first!

6   Be creative – alter angles and distances to see if you can improve the flight pattern.

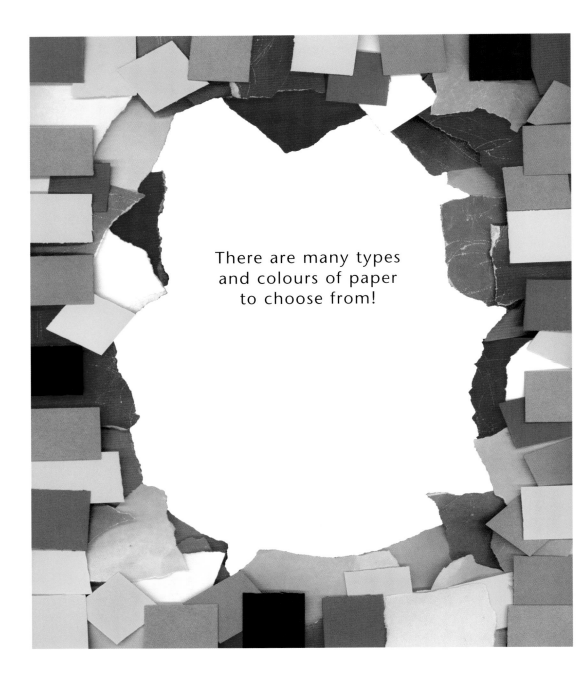

There are many types
and colours of paper
to choose from!

Choosing Paper

The choice of paper patterns is entirely up to you, but be warned that some types of paper (for example, sugar paper) do not make very good planes, since it isn't crisp enough. Some types of paper will absorb moisture from the air more quickly and should be avoided. If the design is very complicated, you may need thinner paper, as above a certain size, the plane simply won't fly at all.

Standard European A4 paper or American photocopy letter size is perfect for most uses and is cheap to buy. Tracing paper is light, but strong, making it great for planes. Here is how you create A4 proportioned paper from a different shaped rectangle or a square.

Introduction

When you fold the more complicated paper planes, you might be in awe of the people who created them. They might seem talented and artistic, but this isn't always the case. Many simply adapt ideas from other designs and add a few new touches. If you start with a simple design, you can alter distances, change some of the angles, add extra creases and miss some creases. Eventually, you'll have an original design!

When testing your designs, carry out test flights after each change to see what effect it had. If it flies properly, you have adapted it successfully. If not, start with a new sheet and try some different changes. Don't keep altering the same model, since the paper will have many unwanted creases. Since paper is so cheap, it will cost very little! If you know someone who works in an office, they probably throw away hundreds of sheets of paper every week. A polite request should get you as much folding material as you need.

Competitions

If you are serious about paper planes, you'll want to challenge some of the world records by entering or setting up competitions. There are a number of categories for which there are international records. These include 'time aloft', (how long can you keep your plane in the air (this is currently over 20 seconds) and 'distance', how far you can make a paper plane travel. (The current record stands at nearly 60 meters). Many professional competitors use small lengths of sticky tape to keep the sides of the plane together. However, there is now an official category for 'origami', where the design must only use folding techniques. World record holders take their hobby very seriously and put in hours of practice, building up the specific muscles that are used to launch a plane. If you want to hold a competition at work or school, all you really need is a large open space with no wind. To attempt a world record, you'll need a large aircraft hangar! You can also organise less serious categories such as acrobatics, most decorative design, worst flyer(!) and most entertaining launch technique.

Societies

Around the world, you'll find small groups of people who are devoted to paper planes. You may have more success by joining origami societies. There is at least one in every major country in the world. You will be able read a regular magazine, buy proper paper and get your hands on books featuring paper planes. Perhaps most importantly, you'll make contact with lots of other people who enjoy paper-folding. People who do origami (the Japanese word for paper-folding) are usually very friendly and will help you with any folding problems you may have. Many origamists are keen paper-plane flyers in their spare time. Here are two of the largest web-sites.

British Origami Society:
www.britishorigami.org.uk
Origami USA www.ousa.com

Introduction

At the time of writing, the current records are:

TIME ALOFT

Guinness World Record

27.6 seconds set by Ken Blackburn 1998

Guinness British Record

20.9 seconds set by Chris Edge & Andy Currey 28th July 1996

Origami Record

20.9 seconds set by Andy Currey 28th July 1996

DISTANCE

Guinness World Record

193 feet (58.8m) set by Tony Fletch 21st May 1985

Guinness British Record

104 feet (31.7m) set by Andy Currey 19th September 1997

Origami Record

94 feet (28.7m) set by Robin Glynne 19th September 1997

Introduction

Glossary of Aviation Terms

Aileron: a moveable part of an aeroplane's wing, which makes an aeroplane roll.

Airfoil: the wing of an aeroplane, which produces lift.

Angle of attack: The angle at which the wings meet the air.

Asymmetrical: a design with wings that are a different shape to each other.

Barnstormer: a plane designed to perform aerobatics.

Canard: a design where the tail is at the front rather than the rear.

Centre of gravity: the point at which a plane balances.

Control surfaces: moveable parts of the plane that control flight.

Elevator: a part of the tail which tilts an aeroplane up or down.

Flight pattern: the path a plane makes through the air.

Fuselage: the main body of the plane.

Laminar-flow wing: a wing that creates less air resistance (drag) than a normal wing.

Leading edges: the front edges of a wing.

Lift: a force which acts on the wings to move the plane upward.

Mach number: mach 1 is the speed of sound.

Pitch: when the tail of the plane moves the up or down.

Trailing edges: the back edges of the wing.

Ornithopter: old-fashioned type of flying machine that looks like a bird.

Rudder: the vertical part of a tail.

Roll: when one wing moves up as the other moves down.

Rate of roll: the speed the aeroplane rolls.

Stable: when a plane flies straight and level without rolling, pitching or yawing.

Stall: when the plane loses control and drops from the sky!

Supersonic: an airplane capable of exceeding the speed of sound.

Swept-wing: a design where leading and trailing edges of a wing point backward.

Unstable: when a plane changes direction without control.

VTOL: Vertical Take Off & Landing - an aircraft that can fly straight upwards.

Yaw: when one wing moves forward as the other moves backwards.

Wing tip: the outer end of an airplane's wing.

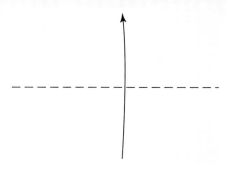

1 Fold one long side to meet the other, adjust until they are perfectly lined up. Hold the layers in position with one hand, then crease firmly and unfold.

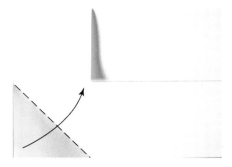

2 Fold the lower left-hand corner in so that the short edge lies along the central crease. The completed fold is shown on the other side.

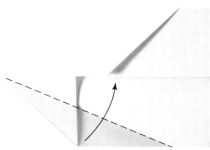

3 Make a similar fold by taking the folded edge to meet the central crease. The completed fold is shown on the other side. Remember to make sharp creases.

4 Fold the plane in half along the central crease to produce this step.

5 Fold the wing tip to meet the original half-way crease. Turn the paper round so that you can fold away from yourself, as this makes life easier.

6 This is the result. Repeat the fold with the other wing.

7 Because this design has a sharp point at one end, it might be dangerous to fly towards people. To make it safer, it's a good idea to cut or tear the sharp point off. You'll be surprised to see that this produces a mini-plane!

8 Complete!

FLIGHT ADVICE

Launch
Medium-strength at a slight upwards angle.

Trim
The wings should have a slight upward angle (dihedral).

Creative suggestions
Try turning the paper over before step 3. Try folding in half using a mountain crease in step 4.

Classic Glider

This is another tried-and-tested design. The idea of 'locking' the flaps together using the triangular tab was first suggested by a Japanese paper plane expert called Eiji Nakamura. When trimmed properly, it is a superb glider, yet it is simple and quick to make.

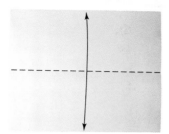

1 Fold one long side to meet the other, crease firmly and unfold.

2 Fold both halves of a short edge to lie along the central crease, as with the Classic Dart. Leave a small 'fudge factor' (see next step).

3 Because paper planes can often be several layers thick, folding in half towards the final stages can be awkward. To help, we often leave a small gap when folding in to the central crease. American folders refer to this as a 'fudge factor'.

4 Fold the end of the triangle to the right, almost to the end of the central crease, leaving a gap about as wide as your thumb (it isn't critical). Refer to the next picture for guidance.

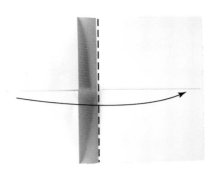

5 Fold a corner to lie along the central crease, but move it slightly to the left before creasing. This creates a small gap on the left-hand side, making it safer to throw in a crowd! The completed fold is shown on the other side

6 Swing the small triangle to the left, overlapping the two corners. This 'locks' them in place during flight.

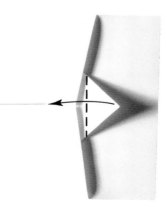

7 Mountain-fold the plane in half, swinging the lower half underneath.

8 This is the result. Turn the paper around.

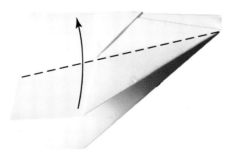

9 Starting at the corner of the blunted nose, fold the wings past the lower edge. Refer to the next picture for guidance.

10 This is the result – the hidden edge is shown in x-ray view. Repeat with the other wing.

FLIGHT ADVICE

Launch
Medium-strength at a slight
upwards angle.

Trim
The wings should have a
slight upward angle
(dihedral).

Creative suggestions

Alter the fold used to create
the wings in step 10,
making the wings firstly
bigger, then smaller. How
does this affect the flight? If
you don't 'lock' the flaps,
does it make a difference?

11 Complete!

Hawk

This is another design with a long history, having been around since at least the 1930s. It uses an elegant series of origami techniques to create the nose section. You should make this design several times until you are confident about the folding method. Start with the central crease in place.

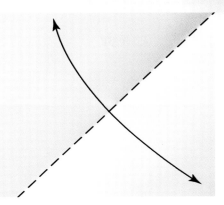

1 Fold a short edge over to meet a long edge. Crease firmly and unfold.

2 Repeat the fold to the other long edge - the picture shows this step before unfolding.

3 Open the paper out. Turn the paper over so that the creases you have made are now mountain folds.

Hawk

4 Fold the corners to meet the ends of the diagonal creases. Crease and unfold.

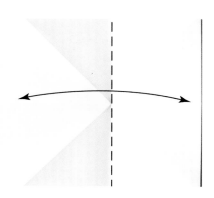

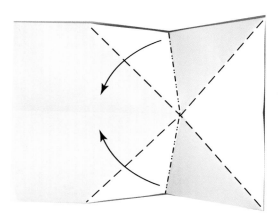

5 Turn the paper over and use the creases to collapse the paper into a triangular shape.

6 This is the result. The triangular section is known as a 'waterbomb base' in the origami world.

7 Fold one of the loose corners to the tip of the triangle.

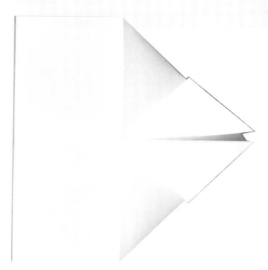

8 Repeat on the other corner. This is the result.

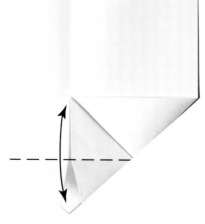

9 Turn the paper around to this position. Fold the two loose corners to the opposite corner of the internal square, taking the layer underneath with them. Crease carefully (due to the thickness) and unfold.

Hawk

10 Turn the paper back to the previous position. Fold one side of the square to meet the horizontal crease. Crease and unfold.

11 Repeat the last step with the lower-right side of the square. Repeat the last two steps on the upper side of the square.

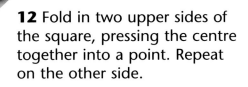

12 Fold in two upper sides of the square, pressing the centre together into a point. Repeat on the other side.

13 Turn the paper over and fold the tip in on an existing crease. The crease is a mountain, which you'll need to change to a valley. Fold carefully and enjoy the way the folds move into position.

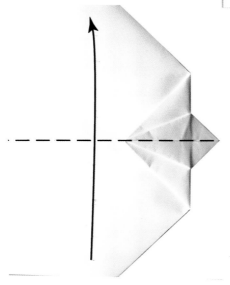

14 This is the result. Valley-fold in half along the central crease.

15 This is the result.

16 Fold one of the wings down, parallel to the lower edge, starting at the top of the nose section.

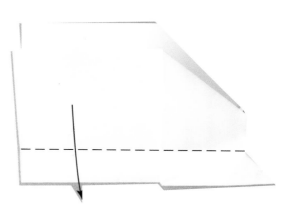

17 Then fold it back up level with the base of the plane.

18 Fold back down once more and repeat with the other wing. You can experiment with the position of these pleats.

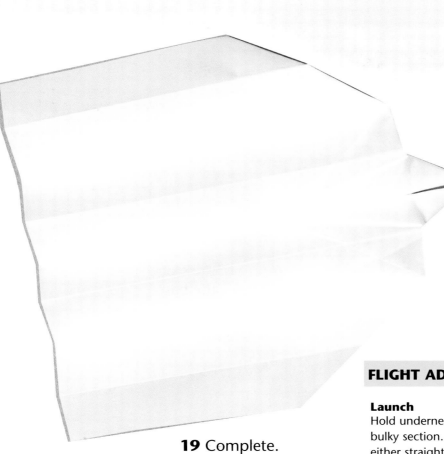

19 Complete.

FLIGHT ADVICE

Launch
Hold underneath by the
bulky section. Launch firmly,
either straight forward or
directly upwards.

Trim
The creases on the wings
should be symmetrical.

Creative suggestions
Try lots of different ways to
crease the wings; add more
creases, also try fewer
creases.

Test Plane

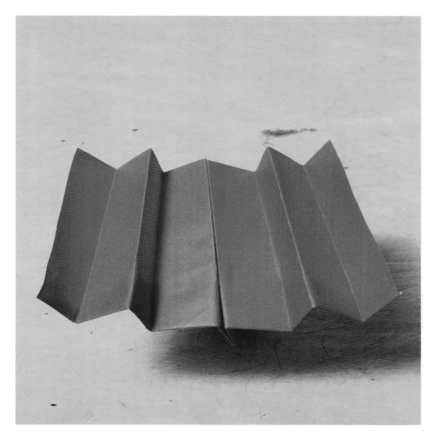

by Nick Robinson

This design will help you explore the effect that various wing configurations can have upon the flight pattern. You can use these ideas when exploring variations of the other designs in the book.

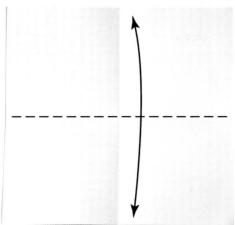

1 Start with a square creased in half. Fold in half, crease and unfold.

2 Fold two corners to the centre, crease and unfold.

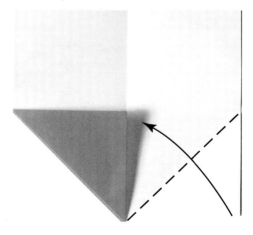

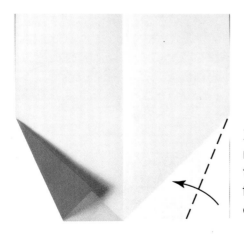

3 Fold two edges in to meet the creases made in the last step. Swing both flaps over on existing creases.

Test Plane

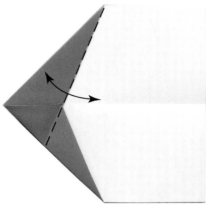

4 Fold one side over along the inside edge. Repeat with the other flap, leaving it in place.

5 Rotate the paper. Follow the creases shown to form a central point, which you swing downwards.

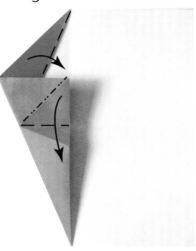

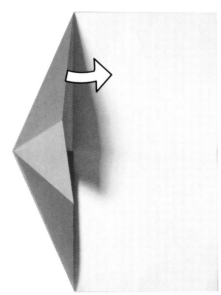

6 Pull out the layer of paper from within the layers.

7 Tuck the layer
underneath.

8 Fold the whole coloured
section over on an existing
crease.

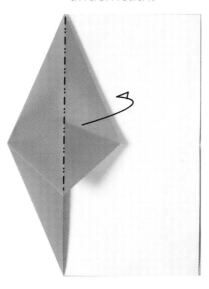

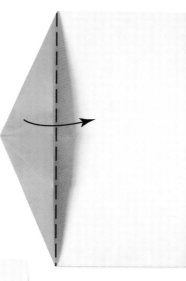

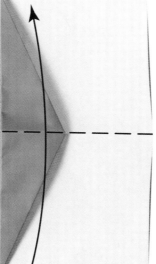

9 Fold the paper
in half.

10 Fold both wings down to form a narrow body.

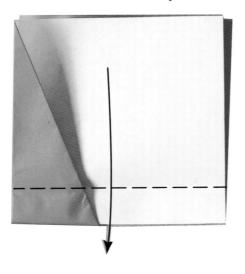

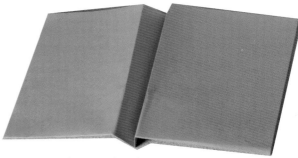

11 This is the basic shape to which you can add variations.

13 Further creases make a more complicated profile.

12 Here, two wingtips have been folded up. Try folding them down and compare.

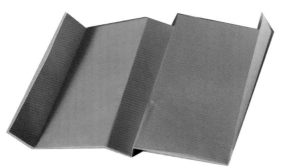

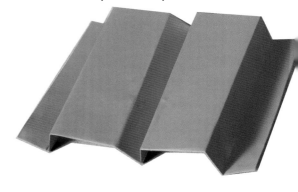

14 You can go as far as you like, but try each step to see if it helps the flight, or hinders it.

FLIGHT ADVICE

Launch
Experiment!

Trim
Experiment!

Creative suggestions
Experiment!

How to hold your plane

Canard

Traditional, arranged by Nick Robinson

This is a well known variation on the traditional dart, where the original corners are allowed to point out instead of being folded away. The term canard (which is French for 'duck') refers to aircraft with some kind of stabilisers at the front end.

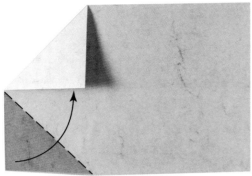

1 Start with an A4 or similar rectangle, creased in half. Fold two corners to the centre.

2 Turn the paper over and take the folded edges to the centre, allowing the corners to pop out again. Unfold these flaps.

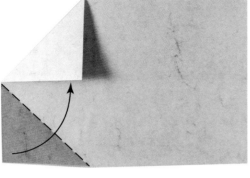

3 Fold the lower left-hand edge to the crease you made in the last step. This step is not used in the traditional design.

4 Refold the flaps on existing creases.

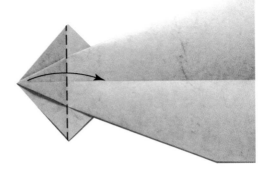

5 Turn the paper over and fold the nose section in half.

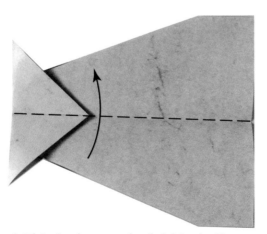

6 This is the result; fold in half.

7 Fold both wings down to the long folded edge.

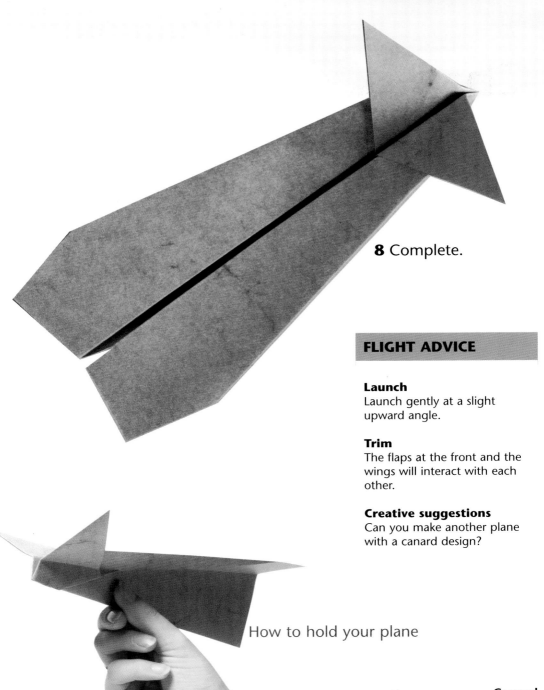

8 Complete.

Launch
Launch gently at a slight upward angle.

Trim
The flaps at the front and the wings will interact with each other.

Creative suggestions
Can you make another plane with a canard design?

How to hold your plane

Championship

Traditional

This is the basic design used by many of the current record-breakers in the paper airplane world, to which they add a strip of tape to keep the wings together. As you will see, it flies beautifully without the tape.

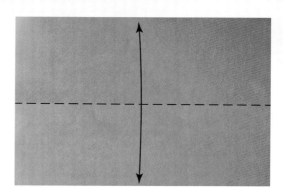

1 Start with an A4 rectangle. Fold one long side to meet the other, crease firmly and unfold.

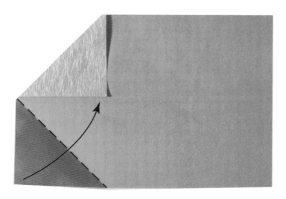

2 Fold the left-hand corners to lie along the central crease. Don't forget a small fudge factor.

3 Fold the triangular shape over along the inside edge.

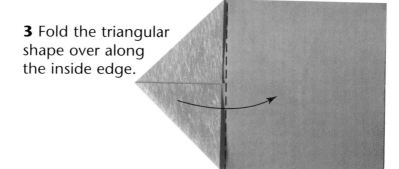

4 Fold two corners in as in step two, then unfold both sides.

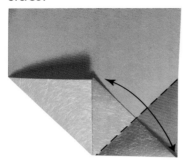

5 Mountain-fold the plane in half. Fold the corner over at a slight angle, starting at the end of the crease. Turn over and match the other side up.

6 Open back to the start of step four. With the small creases in place, refold the existing creases.

7 This is the result. Fold the small triangular flap over to 'lock' the loose flaps, then mountain- fold the plane in half.

8 Mountain-fold the plane in half again. Fold the wings down: the crease starts at the tip of the nose and passes through the top of the tiny triangle.

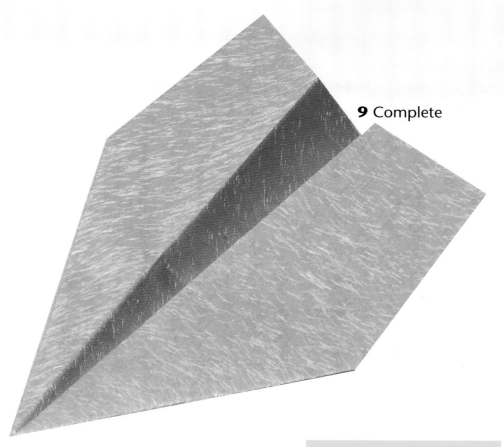

9 Complete

FLIGHT ADVICE

Launch
Launch with a firm forward release, try all different angles of release.

Trim
As ever, adjust the wing angles.

Creative suggestions
Alter the angle at which the wings are folded down in step 8.

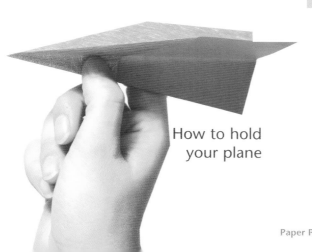

How to hold your plane

Hoop

By Nick Robinson

There are very few circular designs that fly. This one is a variation on a similar traditional design made from a square of paper.

1 Start with a sheet of A4 or similar rectangle. Fold the bottom left corner to meet the top right corner.

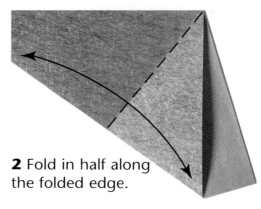

2 Fold in half along the folded edge.

3 Like this. Crease firmly and unfold completely.

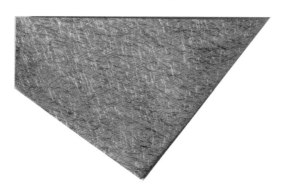

4 You have now created a crease which runs from corner to opposite corner. Fold along that crease.

5 Make a pinch mark to locate the half-way point of the central crease.

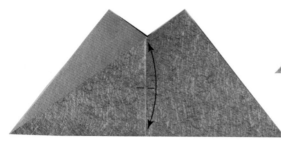

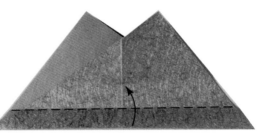

6 Take the folded edge to meet the pinch mark.

7 Carefully fold the outside edge to the inside edge. Crease and unfold.

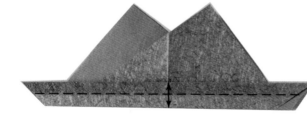

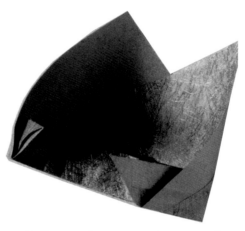

8 Form the paper into a tube and start to feed one end into the other.

9 Finally, refold the crease made in step seven to lock the paper together. Make sure to hold the interlocking flaps together as you start this.

10 Once in place, run your fingers around the edge to make it smooth and circular.

11 Complete.

How to hold your plane

FLIGHT ADVICE

Launch
The thin part of the loop should be on top – hold by the sides or the lower rear end and push it forwards at medium speed.

Creative suggestions
Alter the amount folded in during steps 6 and 7. Try to make the same design starting with a square.

Radford

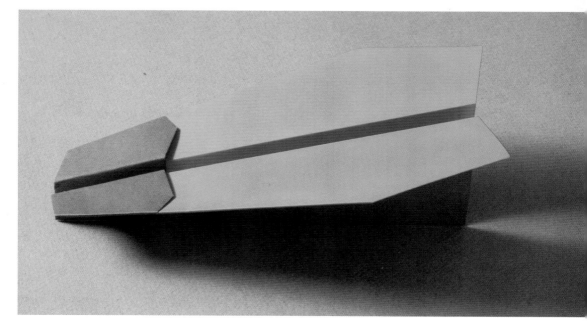

By Nick Robinson

This attractive sequence of folds creates a glider that performs very well. It was named in memory of Mark Radford, an origami friend of the author.

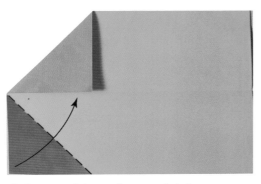

2 Fold the tip in to meet the two corners.

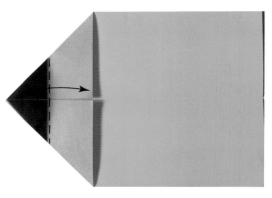

1 Start with a sheet of A4, creased in half. Fold a corner in to lie along the central crease. Repeat with the matching corner.

3 Swing the thicker section back over along the inside raw edges.

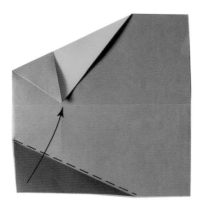

4 Turn the paper over. If you flatten the paper, you'll be able to see the hidden edge underneath. Fold the tips of the thicker section to touch the central crease at this point.

5 Fold the outer edges of the wings to lie along the central crease. Crease and unfold.

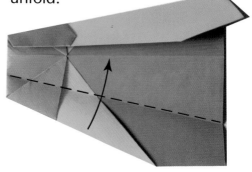

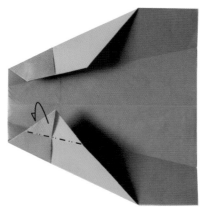

6 Reverse the direction of the creases to fold the small sections underneath.

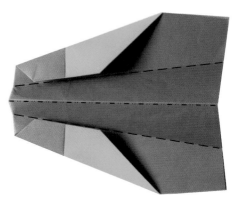

7 Form the classic paper plane profile using existing creases.

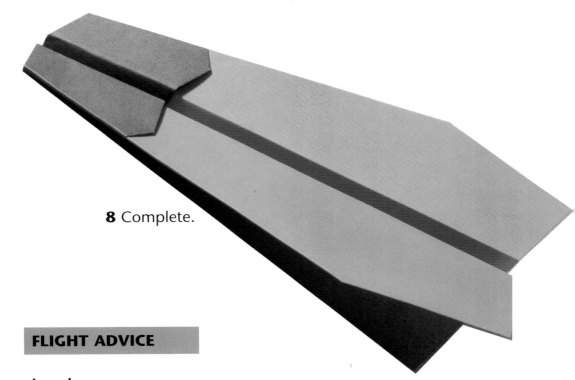

8 Complete.

FLIGHT ADVICE

Launch
Medium-strength at a slight upwards angle.

Trim
The wings should have a slight upward angle (dihedral).

Creative suggestions
Alter the distances in steps 2 and 3.

How to hold your plane

Flying Square

By Nick Robinson

This design is unusual, in that it starts with a square and finishes with a square! The design arranges internal layers of paper towards the front, so that the centre of gravity will allow for a gliding flight.

Flying Square

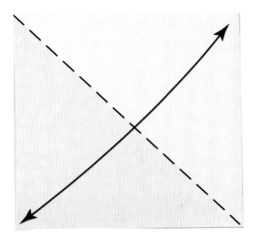

1 Start with a square, white side upwards. Fold in half from corner to corner, crease and unfold.

2 Turn the paper round 90 degrees and fold in half from corner to corner again. The picture shows the finished step.

3 Fold the left-hand corner to the top corner. The completed fold is shown on the right.

4 Fold the right-hand triangle in half towards you. The completed fold is shown on the left.

5 Fold the upper edge of the right-hand triangular section to meet the outside edge. The completed fold is shown on the other side.

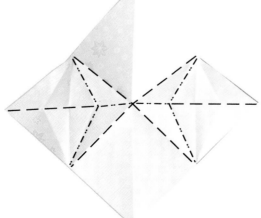

6 Open the paper out completely and turn to the white side. Alter the creases shown to match the direction indicated.

7 Start to form the paper into a 3D shape, bringing the furthest corner towards you. The paper will collapse into a small square. Refer to the next picture for guidance.

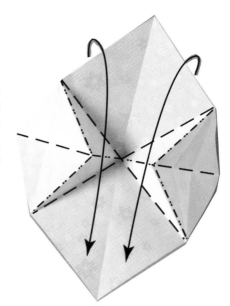

8 This should be the result. If not, unfold and check you have used the correct mountain and valley creases. Use existing creases to fold the small flaps into a pocket.

9 One flap is in place, the other is being tucked in.

10 Curl the edges upwards to complete.

FLIGHT ADVICE

Launch
Hold by the rear corner, above your head and launch with a gentle forward release. Try it from a high building!

Trim
The outer wingtips should be curled upwards.

How to hold your plane

Sallas

By Nick Robinson

This design is named after a talented German creator called Joan Sallas. It starts with a smaller sheet of paper than the usual A4. You can also try many of the other designs in the book from smaller paper, to see how they perform.

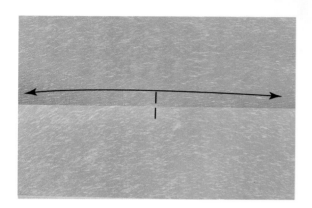

1 Start with a sheet of A5 (half A4) or similar rectangle, creased in half. Fold the short edges together, pinching the centre point.

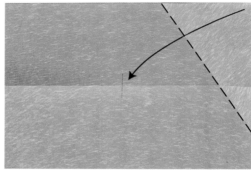

2 Fold a corner to lie exactly on the centre point.

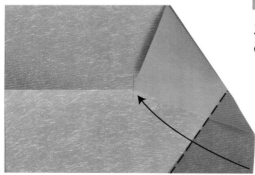

3 Repeat with the other corner.

Sallas

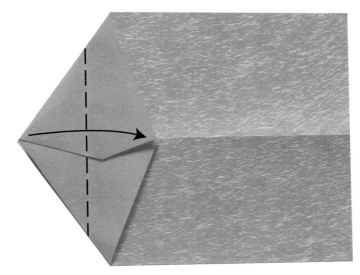

4 Now fold the tip to the same place.

5 Turn the paper over, then fold each half of the short edge to the central crease.

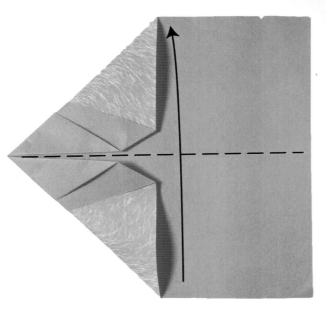

6 Fold the plane in half.

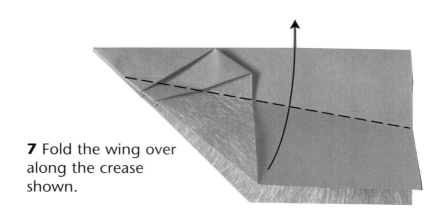

7 Fold the wing over
along the crease
shown.

Sallas

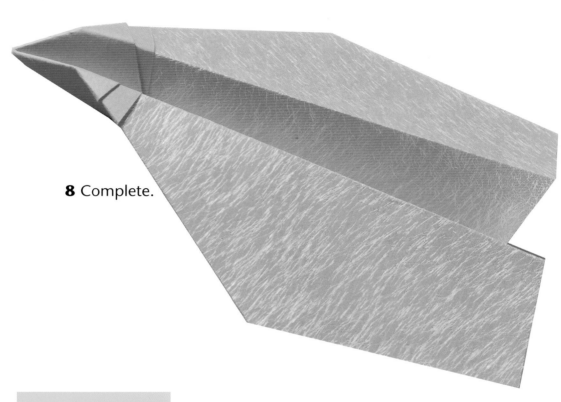

8 Complete.

FLIGHT ADVICE

Launch
Moderate speed, straight
forward.

Trim
Keep the wings almost
horizontal.

Creative suggestions
Alter the angles of the
wings.

How to hold
your plane

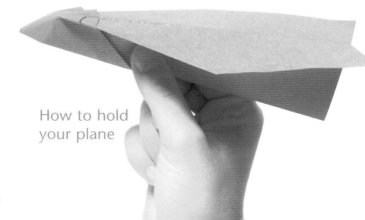

Triplane

By Nick Robinson

Unlike most paper planes, this design uses a 60 degree geometry. It is quite easy to create this angle and there will be many exciting designs waiting to be discovered using these techniques.

1 Start with a square, folded in half. Fold in both sides to the central crease.

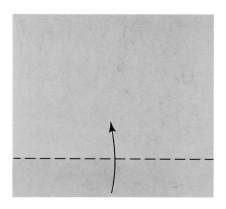

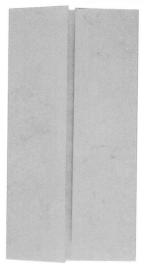

2 This is the result. Turn the paper over.

3 Fold one edge to the central crease and make a gentle crease about one third the length of the paper.

Triplane

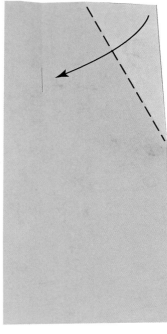

4 Make a crease that starts in the middle of the short edge. The corner you fold in should just touch the crease you made in the last step.

5 Rotate the paper and fold the other corner to lie along the crease made in the last step.

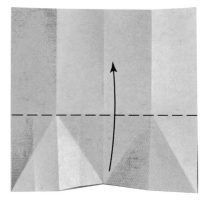

6 Open the paper out fully: you can see the 60 degree triangles formed. Fold in making your crease pass through the inside corners of the triangles.

7 Using existing creases, fold one corner in, flattening the outside point.

9 Pull out a layer of paper to tuck the point within a pocket underneath.

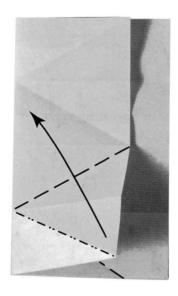

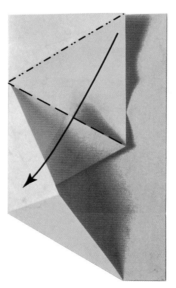

8 Repeat the move with the other corner.

Triplane

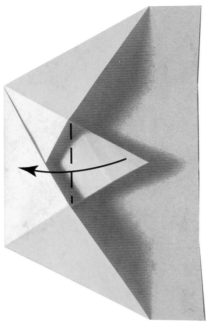

11 Take the folded front edge of the wing to lie along the centre. Repeat with the other wing.

10 Fold the point over.

12 Form the classic plane profile to complete the design.

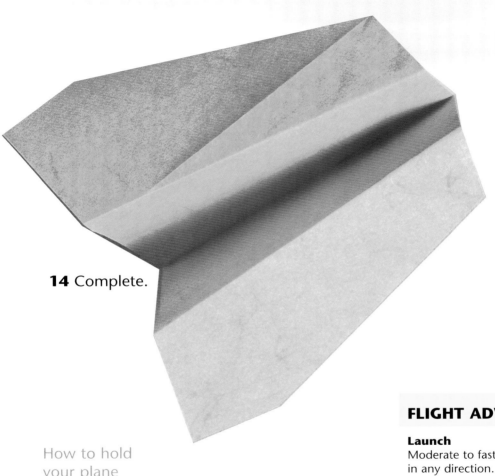

14 Complete.

How to hold
your plane

FLIGHT ADVICE

Launch
Moderate to fast speed,
in any direction.

Trim
Adjust the wing angles.

Creative suggestions
Start at step six and
design a new plane of
your own!

The Alison

By Nick Robinson

This is a slow, stable glider, which doesn't use the familiar 'short sides to the centre' technique of many planes. Instead, the paper is folded in half, then half of the paper is tucked back into the nose section to generate the proper centre of gravity.

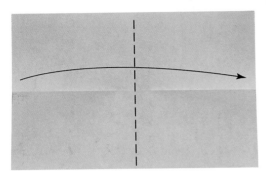

1 Start with a sheet of A4 or similar rectangle, creased in half between the long edges.Fold the two short edges together.

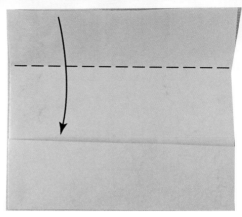

2 Fold the raw edges to the central crease.

3 Fold the short edges of the left-hand layers back to the long edges, crease and unfold.

4 Swing open the first of the layers, pressing the top corner into a triangle, using existing creases.

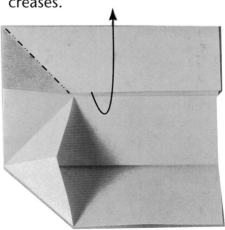

The Alison

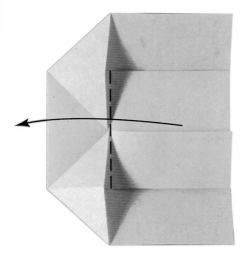

5 Swing the central section to the left.

6 Fold the lower edge to touch the upper edge of the section you have just folded. Repeat other side.

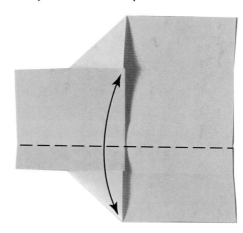

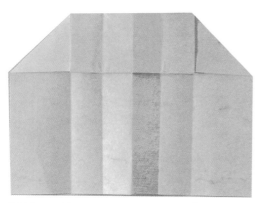

7 Turn the paper over and fold the smaller flap over the folded edge, crease and unfold to step five.

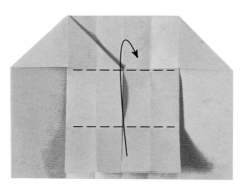

8 Using the creases you added in steps five and seven, tuck the central flap into the pocket.

9 Refold the central crease through the nose section and adjust the profile to that shown in the final image.

FLIGHT ADVICE

Launch
Hold the plane gently by the centre. Launch with a gentle forward push.

Trim
Adjust the various angles of the wings.

Creative suggestions
Can you find an imaginative way of using the 'spare' paper in step eight?

How to hold your plane

Stump

By Nick Robinson

This is another example of how a traditional design can be worked upon to incorporate new ideas. Here, some of the surplus paper at the nose end is overlapped to lock the nose section together and make the design more stable in flight.

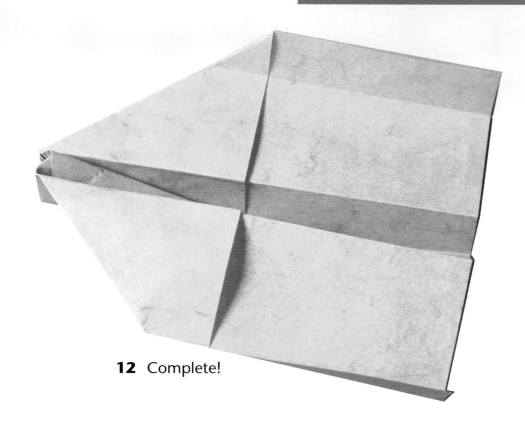

12 Complete!

Launch
Gentle to moderate
speed, directly forward.

Trim
Adjust the wing angles.

Creative suggestions
Try radical changes to the
wing profile.

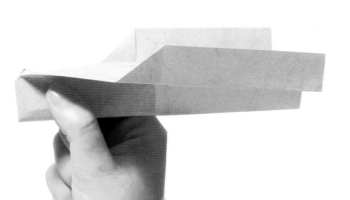

Star Fighter

By Nick Robinson

This design makes use of the two layers of paper created in the first step to create double-sided wingtips. There are very few designs which create this type of wing profile – why not try to create one of your own?

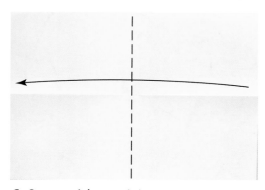

1 Start with an A4 or similar rectangle, creased in half. Fold the two short edges together.

2 Take each half of the folded edge to the centre, crease firmly and unfold.

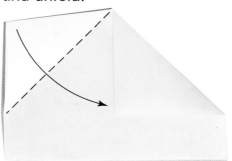

3 Fold the edge to the crease made in the last step, then unfold again.

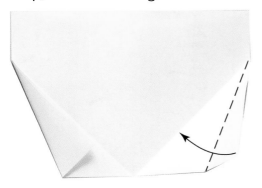

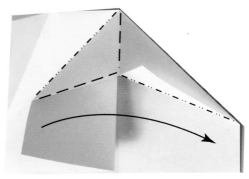

4 Alter the creases as necessary, making the longest one a mountain and the shorter one a valley, on both layers of paper. If you then re-form the creases, the paper will collapse into the position shown. Look at the picture closely!

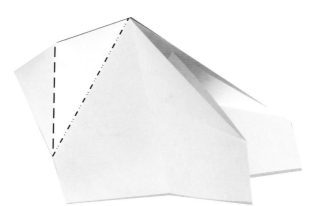

5 Repeat on the other wing.

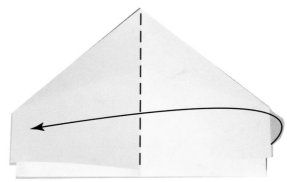

6 Fold the whole model in half.

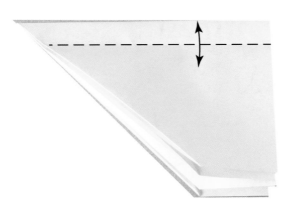

7 Make a crease to form the body. The exact position isn't critical. You can also do this in two stages by folding each wing separately.

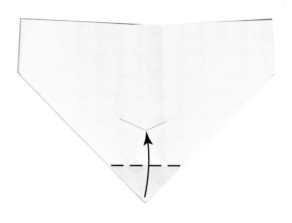

8 Fold the tip of the nose to the point where the hidden layers meet inside.

9 Swing the flap over once more.

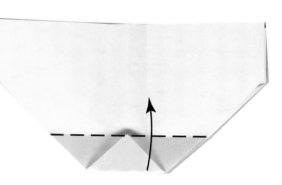

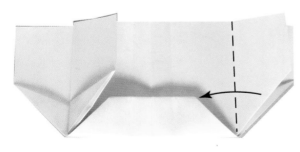

10 Use the edges of the nose section as a reference to fold the sides of the wings to. You should repeat this on the three other flaps.

Star Fighter

11 Open out into the profile shown. Complete.

FLIGHT ADVICE

Launch
Launch at speed, at most angles.

Trim
Keep the wings at right angles to the body, adjust the wing tips symmetrically.

Creative suggestions
Try alternative wing profiles.

How to hold your plane

Landscape

By Nick Robinson

This plane is so called because unlike most paper airplanes, it uses a sheet of paper which is in the 'landscape' format (wider than high). Most designs start with the paper in 'portrait' format. If you are wanting to create truly original designs, this layout is more likely to get you results!

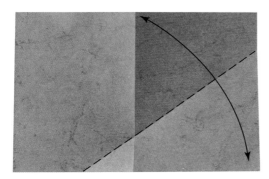

1 Start with a sheet of A4 or similar rectangle, creased in half between the short edges. Take the bottom right corner to the top centre, crease firmly and unfold.

2 Fold the outside edge to the crease you have just made, crease and unfold.

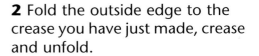

3 Repeat step one on the left-hand side.

4 Make a valley fold from the bottom left corner to the end of the crease on the upper surface.

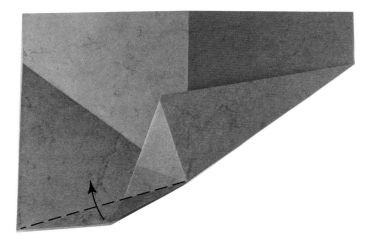

5 Make a fold similar to step two on the left-hand side.

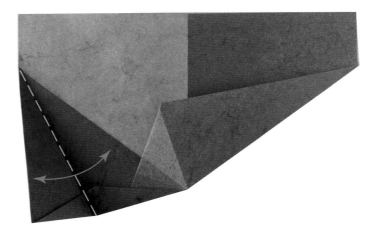

6 Using the existing creases, swing the paper over and tuck it underneath the layers on the right.

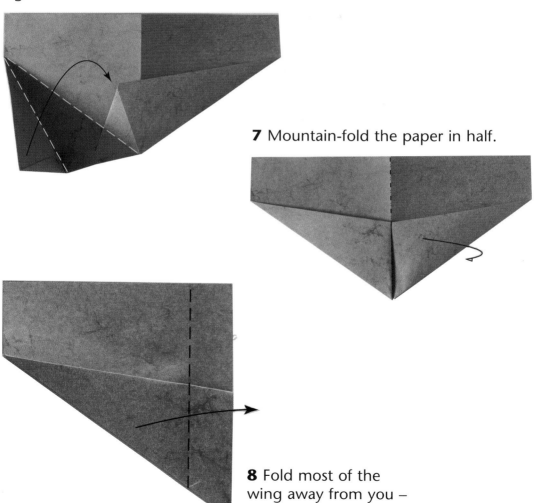

7 Mountain-fold the paper in half.

8 Fold most of the wing away from you – the exact distance isn't critical.

9 Fold the wing back at a slight angle so that the corner of the wing-tip is behind the rear edge of the plane.

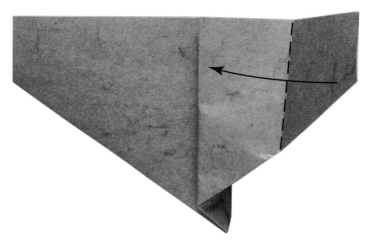

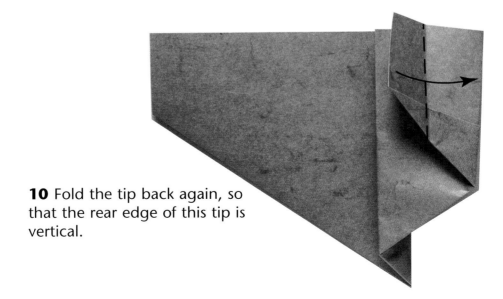

10 Fold the tip back again, so that the rear edge of this tip is vertical.

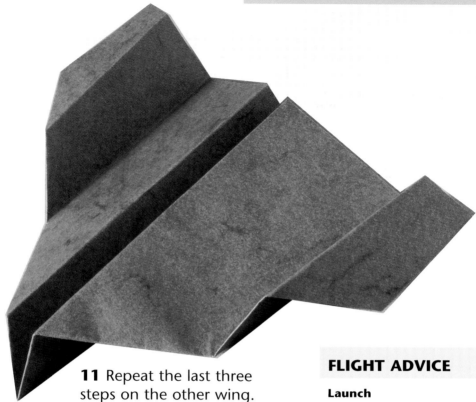

11 Repeat the last three steps on the other wing.

How to hold your plane

FLIGHT ADVICE

Launch
Open the wings to match the final photograph. Launch with medium strength at a slight upwards angle.

Trim
The end section of the wings should be at the same angle as the largest wing section.

Creative suggestions
Starting at step 8, create your own design!

Lock Glider

By Nick Robinson

The body (or fuselage) of most paper airplanes tends to open during flight. However, using some origami ingenuity, it is possible to lock the nose together to prevent this.

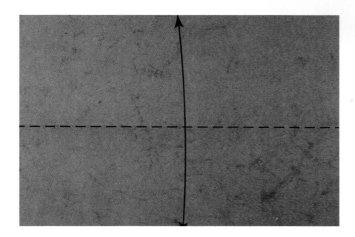

1 Start with an A4 or similar rectangle. Fold the two long sides together, crease and unfold.

2 Fold the two left-hand corners in to the centre crease. Leave a slight fudge factor.

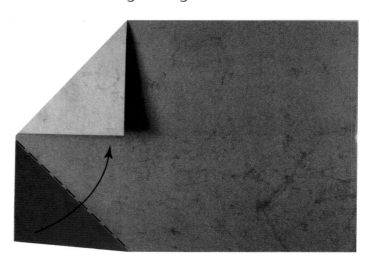

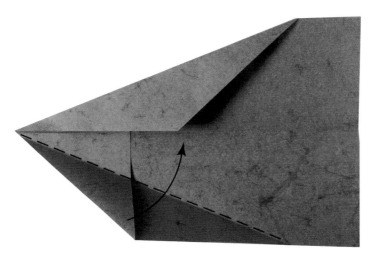

3 Now fold the wings in once more, as in the traditional Dart. Unfold again.

4 Fold part of the raw edge to lie along the crease made in the last step.

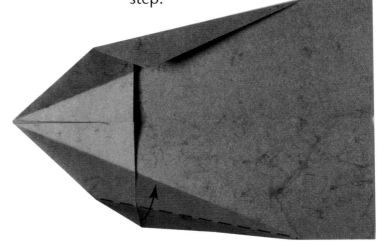

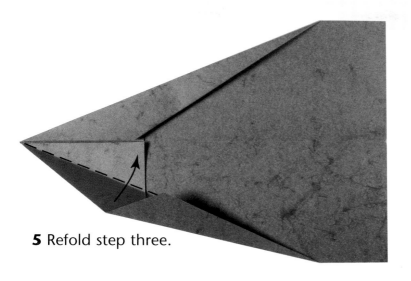

5 Refold step three.

6 Fold the edges of the nose section to lie along the centre crease, but only crease from the tail section as far as the folded edges.

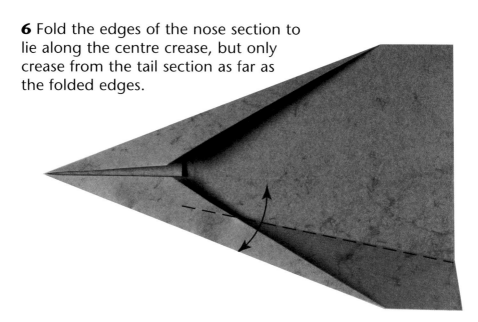

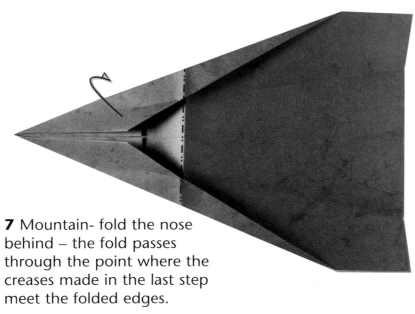

7 Mountain- fold the nose behind – the fold passes through the point where the creases made in the last step meet the folded edges.

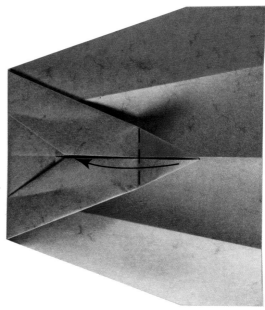

8 Turn the paper over. Fold the sharp tip back to the inside of the triangular section.

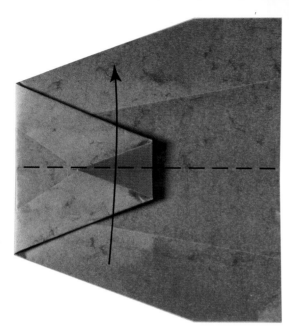

9 Valley-fold the whole plane in half.

10 Fold the tip of the nose over along an inside edge – you should be able to both see and feel this edge. Crease and unfold.

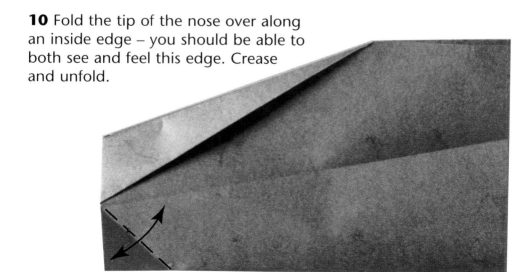

Lock Glider

11 Open the top of the plane and push the triangular flap inside using the crease you made in the last step. Lift the left-hand flap up and tuck the paper underneath.

12 In progress...

13 ...the step complete. You should be able to refold the plane in half again, with the nose section locked.

14 Complete.

How to hold
your plane

FLIGHT ADVICE

Launch
Medium-strength, at a slight
upwards angle.

Trim
Alter the angle of the wings
to the body. Make sure the
rear corners of the wings are
not curled up or down.

Creative suggestions
In step 6, make a fold at
right angles to the tail to
create a thin, equal body
shape. Continue as before.
This variation should be a
slow glider.

Needle Dart

By Nick Robinson

This is an ultra-modern design, sleek and stylish. It uses the 'squash' technique taken from traditional origami.

1 Start with an A4 rectangle or similar, creased in half.Fold two corners to the centre.

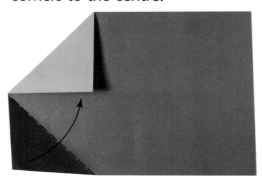

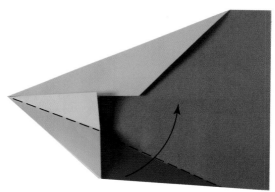

3 Turn the paper over and fold the edges of the sharp end to the centre. These creases only need to extend about one third of the length.

2 Take the folded edges to the centre as well.

Needle Dart

4 Fold the tip to the centre of the opposite end.

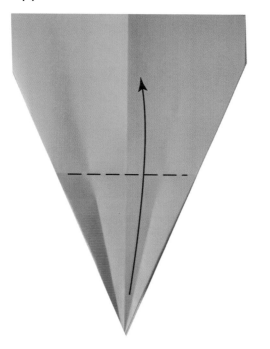

5 Fold the same point back along the hidden inside edges formed in step one.

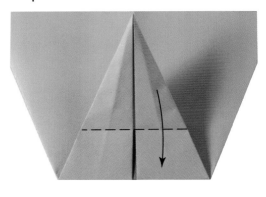

6 Fold the edges of the pointed flap in to the centre, carefully squashing the paper at the end. See the next picture for guidance. Repeat with the other side.

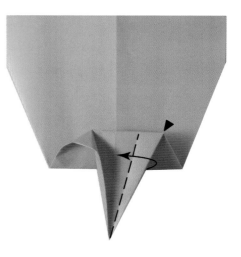

7 Fold the short edge underneath the point in half.

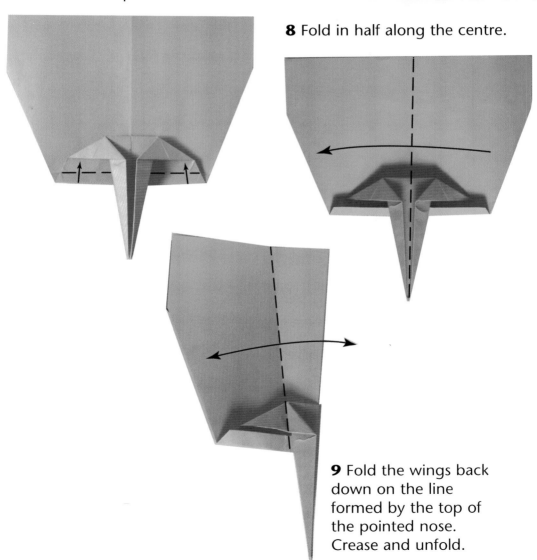

8 Fold in half along the centre.

9 Fold the wings back down on the line formed by the top of the pointed nose. Crease and unfold.

Needle Dart

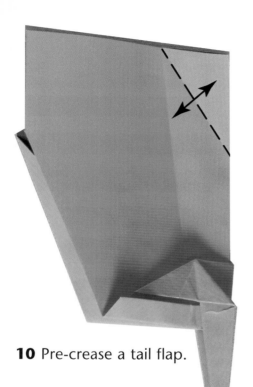

10 Pre-crease a tail flap.

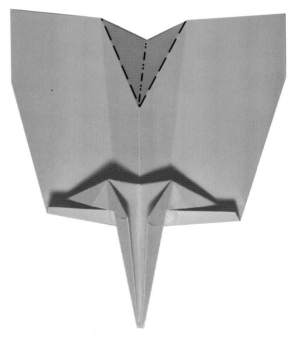

11 Push the tail inside the body, so it sticks out the other side.

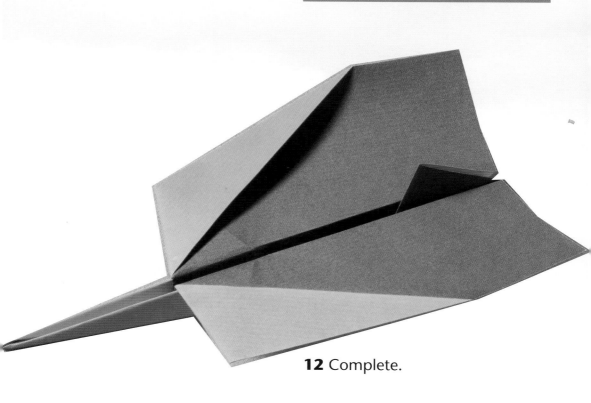

12 Complete.

How to hold
your plane

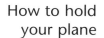

Launch
A steady speed, slightly
upwards.

Trim
As ever, the wings.

Creative suggestions
Try alternative wing
profiles.

The Swift

By Kunihiko Kasahara

Kasahara is one of the foremost origami designers in the world. Here, he turns his skills to creating a highly acrobatic stunt plane, which swoops and turns just like a swift in flight.

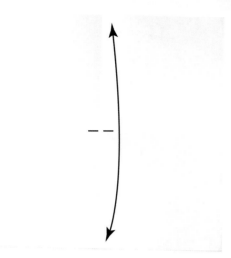

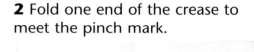

2 Fold one end of the crease to meet the pinch mark.

1 Start with a square, creased in half. Fold one end of the crease to the other, pinching lightly to find the centre point.

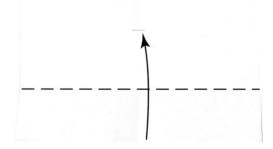

3 Fold both corners over to meet the inside raw edge.

4 Fold each half of the nearest (folded) edge to lie along the vertical centre crease. Leave a slight fudge factor.

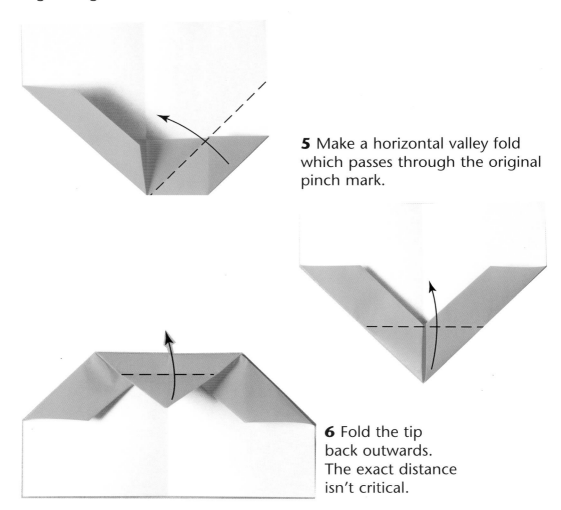

5 Make a horizontal valley fold which passes through the original pinch mark.

6 Fold the tip back outwards. The exact distance isn't critical.

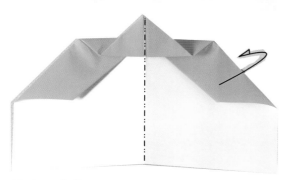

7 Carefully mountain-fold in half on the original central crease.

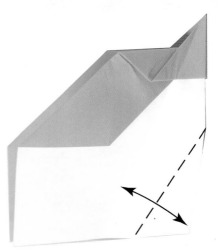

8 Make a crease which starts at the half-way point of the raw edge on the right and passes through the internal angle formed by the coloured sections. Make sure you have this clear in your mind before folding! Repeat with the other wing.

9 Pre-crease a valley fold which will form the tail fin.

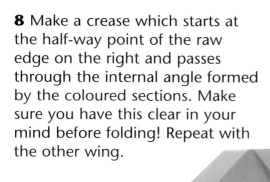

The Swift

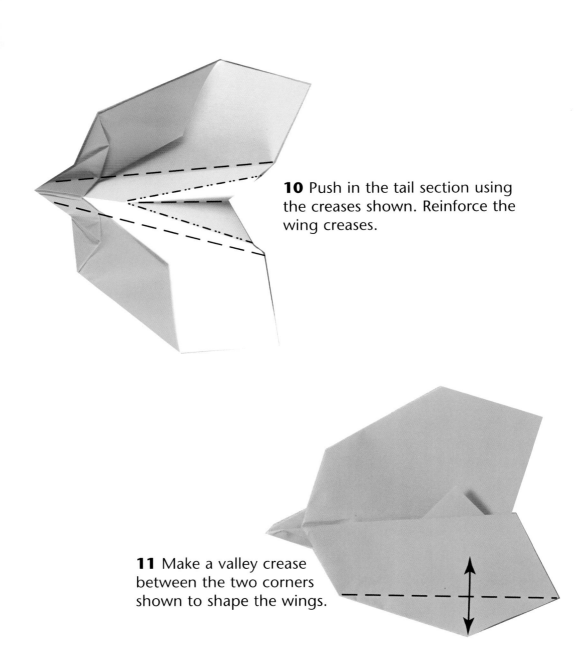

10 Push in the tail section using the creases shown. Reinforce the wing creases.

11 Make a valley crease between the two corners shown to shape the wings.

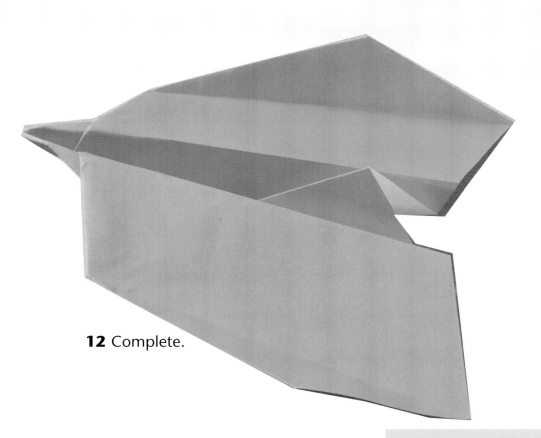

12 Complete.

FLIGHT ADVICE

Launch
AS fast as possible, straight upwards!

Trim
Alter the relative angle of the wings to the wingtips.

Creative suggestions
Try folding the wingtips down instead of up.

The Martin

By Rikki Donachie

This is a very clever design, with a neat, flowing sequence. It ends up with two small flaps with which you can use to launch it.

1 Start with a sheet of A4 creased in half. Fold two corners to the central crease at one end.

2 Take each folded edge to the inside raw edge, creasing as far as the centre.

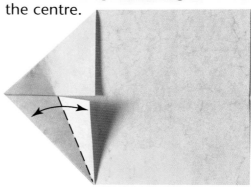

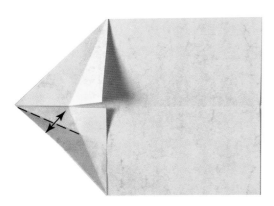

3 Take each folded edge to the centre, creasing as far as the previous fold.

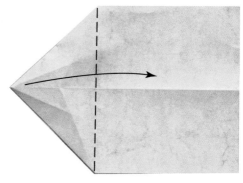

4 Turn the paper over and fold the triangular section over.

The Martin

5 Use existing creases to flatten the paper into a point. Two small mountain creases are formed as you flatten the paper.

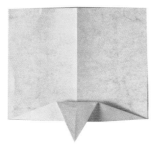

6 This is the result. Turn the paper over.

7 Fold the two outside corners to the centre.

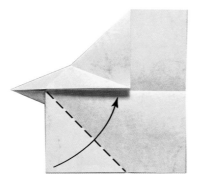

8 Fold the model in half from side to side.

9 Fold the wings over, bisecting the angle of the nose.

10 Fold out two small flaps, with which you can launch the plane.

7 his is the result - fold one layer upwards, turn the paper over and repeat on the matching flap.

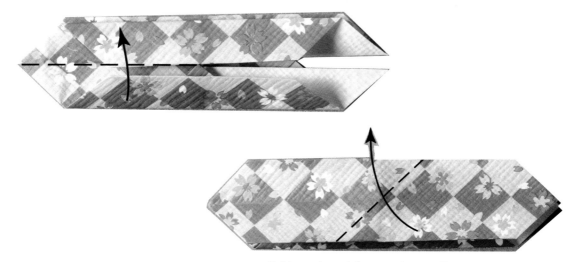

8 You should now have flat sections of paper top and bottom. Fold one of the loose flaps over at 45 degrees.

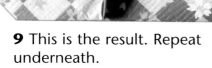

9 This is the result. Repeat underneath.

Spinner

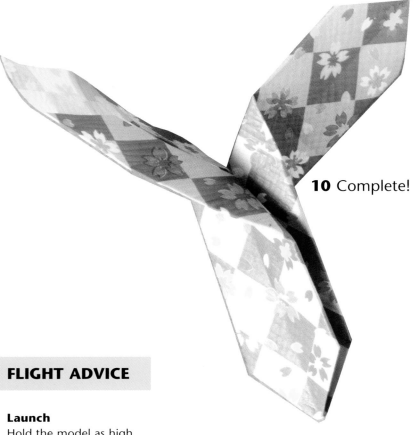

10 Complete!

FLIGHT ADVICE

Launch
Hold the model as high as
possible and release.

Trim
Adjust the angles of the
'wing' flaps.

Creative suggestions
Try making the flaps
wider or more narrow.

How to hold
your plane

Art Deco Wing

By Michael LaFosse

This is a flying wing design, something that is quite hard to achieve using paper. LaFosse is a highly gifted creator and has produced many stunning origami pieces, as well as many unusual and interesting flying designs.!

1 Start with a square of paper. Fold from corner to corner.

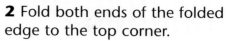

2 Fold both ends of the folded edge to the top corner.

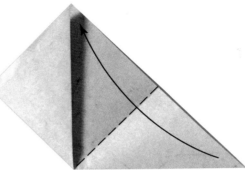

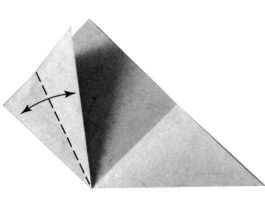

3 Take the left-hand vertical edge to the outside edge, crease and unfold.

4 Lift and squash using the crease you have just made.

5 Repeat on the other side.

6 Turn the paper over and fold the large triangular flap over.

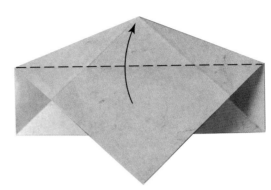

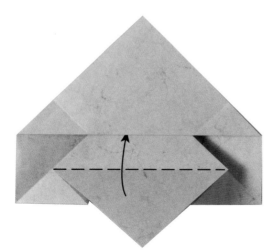

7 Fold the smaller triangular flap upwards, tucking it into the pocket.

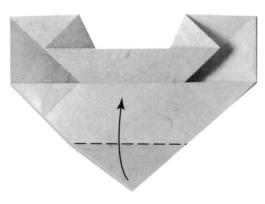

8 Rotate the paper to the position shown. Fold the triangular flap in half.

9 Fold the same section in half again.

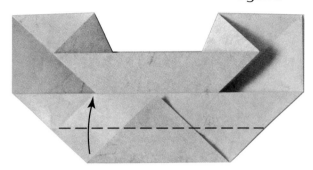

10 Swing the flap over again.

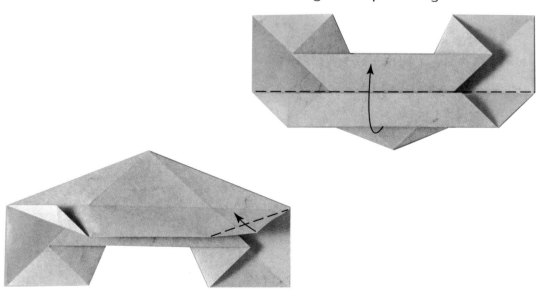

11 Rotate the paper. Fold the two small outside corners to lie along the horizontal edge.

12 Rotate the paper once more. Tuck the flap inside the pocket.

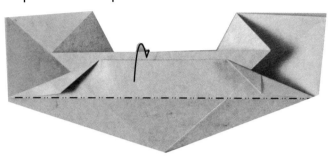

13 Again, rotate the paper. Getting dizzy? Lift the central flap and fold it upwards. At the same time, fold the paper on either side inwards, allowing it to flatten neatly. Check the next picture for help.

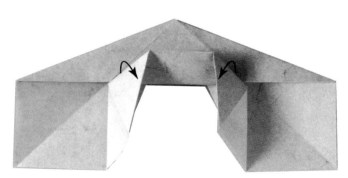

14 This is the result - tuck the paper into the pocket underneath.

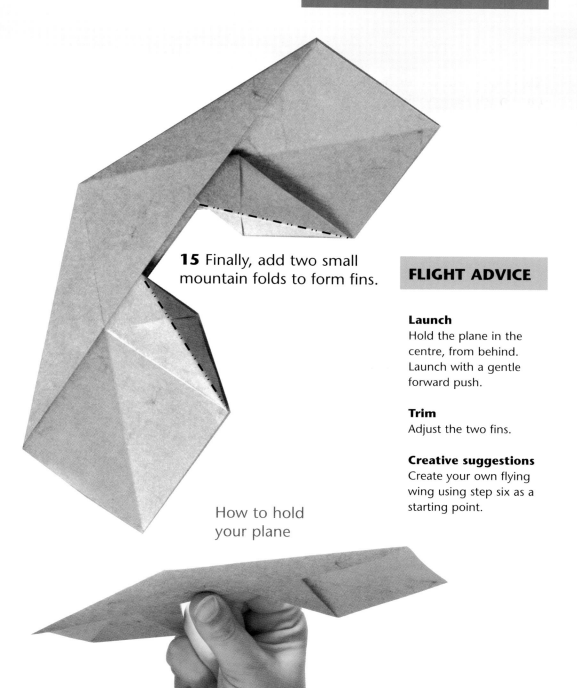

15 Finally, add two small mountain folds to form fins.

FLIGHT ADVICE

Launch
Hold the plane in the centre, from behind. Launch with a gentle forward push.

Trim
Adjust the two fins.

Creative suggestions
Create your own flying wing using step six as a starting point.

How to hold your plane

Rocket

by Nick Robinson

Identical in shape to an existing non-flying design, this fold actually flies. You can also have fun placing a box in the garden, then trying to drop the rocket into it from as far away as possible.

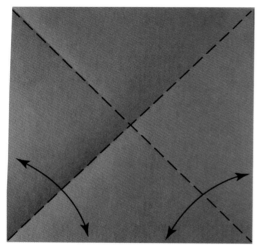

1 Start with a large square of paper. Crease both diagonals.

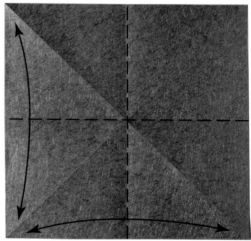

2 Turn the paper over and fold in half from side to side, both ways.

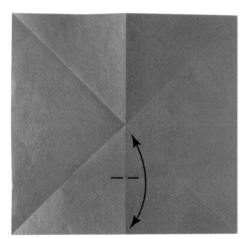

3 Turn back over and add a small crease marking the half-way point.

Rocket

4 Fold the central crease to touch the mark made in the last step. Crease right across the paper.

5 Repeat on all four corners to produce this crease pattern. Turn the paper over.

14 Take one of the folded edges to the vertical centre edge, crease firmly and unfold.

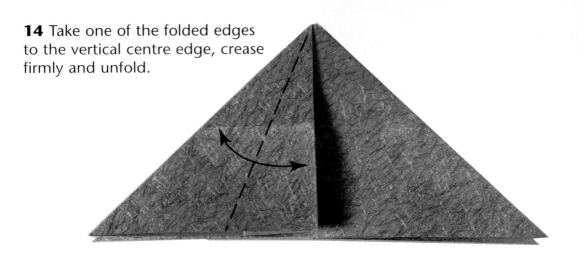

15 Swing the corner up and right, starting at the centre of the lower edge. The crease passes through a meeting point of two creases (shown in grey). See the next picture for guidance.

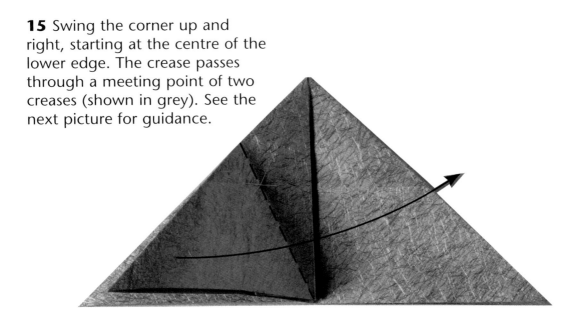

Rocket

16 Collapse the paper using the creases indicated. Once again, use the next picture as a guide.

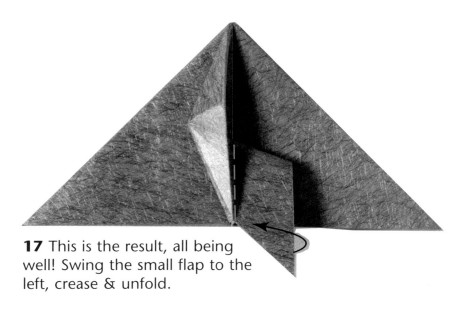

17 This is the result, all being well! Swing the small flap to the left, crease & unfold.

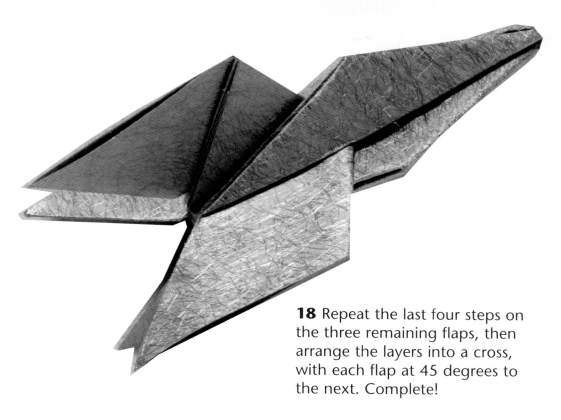

18 Repeat the last four steps on the three remaining flaps, then arrange the layers into a cross, with each flap at 45 degrees to the next. Complete!

How to hold your plane

FLIGHT ADVICE

Launch
This design should be thrown as hard as possible at about 45 degrees. A higher angle will produce a shorter distance.

The Twin

By Nick Robinson

This shows how, with a bit of imagination, exciting new designs can be developed from existing ones. This one uses the Landscape (page 52) and Canard (page 30) designs and with minor adaptations, joins them into a flying model you couldn't achieve using a single sheet.

Start with the Landscape design folded up to step seven, then unfolded completely and the Canard folded to completion, then unfolded to step five.

1 Make a horizontal crease which joins the main crease intersections on either side.

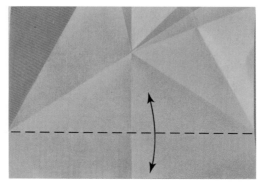

2 Fold the lower corners over so that their inside edges meet the two existing creases.

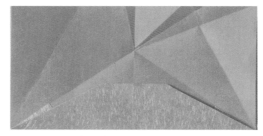

3 Swing the lower section over on the crease made in step one.

4 Take the Canard and fold the tip of the upper square in half towards you. Then mountain-fold the rest of it behind on an existing (valley) crease.

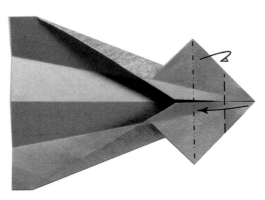

5 Slide the same flap behind the layer of the Landscape section and start to reform the wing creases of the Landscape.

6 Reform another fold.

7 Reform the right- hand section, tucking the paper within, as on the original design.

8 Reform the main body creases of the Canard, extending the creases through the extra paper of the Landscape.

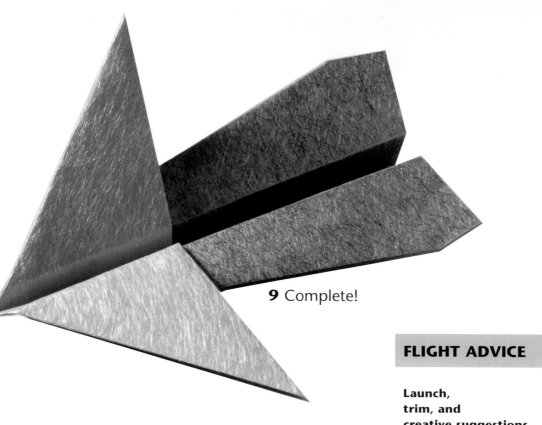

9 Complete!

FLIGHT ADVICE

**Launch,
trim, and
creative suggestions**
By now, I hope you can
work these out for
yourselves!

How to hold
your plane

Index

A

Adjustment 10, 12
Airpane 7
Alison 86
Art Deco Wing 138
Aviation terms 24

C

Canard 52
Championship 56
Competitions 11, 21

D

Dart, classic 8, 28
Dart, needle 116
Designs 20
Dihedral 12
Donachie, Rikki 128

E

Edge, trailing 12
Extras 16

F

Flaps 10, 16
Flight 8
Flying square 69

G

Glider, classic 32
Glider, Lock 108

H

Hawk 38
Hoop 60

K

Kasahara, Kunihiko 122

L

LaFosse, Michael 138
Landscape 102
Launching 11
- angle 11
- locations 15
- speed 12

Credits

Thanks to: Sarah and David King and Colin Bowling.
To Michael LaFosse, Rikki Donachie, Kunihiko Kasahara and Robin Glynn for allowing their designs to be published. Alison, Daisy, Nick, Gomez, Matilda, Big Dave and Bob, all part of my extended family. John, Mick and Joe for helping keep my fingers flexible. To paper-folders everywhere for their fellowship and inspiration and willingness to share ideas; and Ken Blackburn for pushing paper airplane records to the limit and beyond!

The Author: Nick Robinson

An IT lecturer, web author and writer, Nick lives in Sheffield, England. He has been folding for over twenty years and is a council member of the British Origami Society. He also maintains their web site and edits their magazine. He has appeared on television in the UK and abroad and has created numerous designs for magazine, television and other media. Over 150 of his original origami creations have been published in 15 countries around the world. His website is www.12testing.net. As a former professional musician he still performs live, solo improvised ambient guitar concerts.

Additional Picture Credits:

Image p6 © Stockbyte.

Pictures p23, 32, 79, 102, and 137 by Paul Stewart-Reed.